The Michigan Counting Book

Written by Kathy-jo Wargin and Illustrated by Michael Glenn Monroe

Sleeping Bear Press
310 North Main Street
P.O. Box 20
Chelsea, MI 48118
www.sleepingbearpress.com

Printed and bound in Canada.

10 9 8 7 6 5 4 3 2 1

Library of Congress Cataloging-in-Publication Data on file.
ISBN: 1-58536-003-1

To Jake Peter Wargin. You will
always be number one to me.

K.J.W.

To my brother, Rick. I can
always count on you.

M.G.M.

The Kirtland's Warbler is a small songbird with a yellow breast. It favors being low in pine trees or on the ground. The warbler likes to eat ants and caterpillars as well as some plants. It breeds in the northern part of the lower peninsula, and is an endangered species, partly because it will only nest in large stands of young jack pine trees, preferably 80 acres or larger. The Kirtland's Warbler will lay 4 or 5 eggs in its nest in the late spring/early summer, and it takes 14 days for the eggs to mature and hatch.

1 Kirtland's Warbler
he's a sunny fellow!
Singing such a pretty song
with a chest so yellow.

1

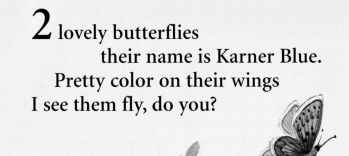

2 lovely butterflies
their name is Karner Blue.
Pretty color on their wings
I see them fly, do you?

The Karner Blue butterfly is a Michigan endangered species. When they are caterpillars, they feed only on wild lupine plant leaves. Because of this limitation, there are not many areas where they can survive. Beautiful butterflies, the male is silver to dark-blue and the female is a gray-brown with portions of blue and orange along its black border. Can you count its wings?

Michigan was the first state to establish a picnic table along its roadsides. The very first table was placed along a highway right-of-way in 1929 on Old U.S. 16 in Ionia County. The table was made from old salvaged planks that were once used as guardrails. The idea was adopted by the state highway department, and many more were placed along major roads in the state. Eventually, other states began to emulate Michigan's wonderful symbol of hospitality.

3 roadside picnic tables
all set up for lunch.
Apples, carrots, peanuts
make a picnic fun to munch!

You can count
  now look, there's more!
    Just turn the page for number...

4 Soo Locks
     going up and going down,
helping boats along the river,
     in and out of town.

The Soo Locks help boats pass over a section of water called the St. Mary's Rapids, on the St. Mary's River, where the water falls nearly 21 feet from Lake Superior to the level of the lower Great Lakes. The Locks raise and lower boats traveling in each direction, allowing safe passage. The first lock was built in 1797, on the Canadian side, by the Northwest Fur Company. This lock was destroyed in the War of 1812. In 1853, The Fairbanks Scale Company began building new locks, and within 2 years, built 2 new locks, each 350 feet long. In May of 1855, they became property of the State of Michigan. In 1881, the locks were transferred to the U.S. Army Corps of Engineers, and today there are 4 locks. How many boats do you see in this picture?

4

The Gray Wolf is an endangered species in the state of Michigan. They are scattered throughout the upper peninsula as well as Isle Royale, where their population continues to grow. Wolf pups are born in mid-to-late April, and most litters average about 4 to 6 pups. In 1989, there were only 2 wolves reported in the upper peninsula, compared to 174 reported in 1999, ten years later.

5

5 howling gray wolves
running in a pack.
The leader is in front
and a small one is in back.

The Dwarf Lake Iris, a threatened species in Michigan, is a miniature iris. It has beautiful blue-purple flowers with yellow splashes of color. Each flower is about 1 to 2 inches in width and height, and the stems are less than 2 inches tall. The Dwarf Lake Iris grows in the Great Lakes region near the north shores of Lakes Huron and Michigan. This delicate flower favors sand and thin soil, and can be found along beach ridges or open dunes. The Dwarf Lake Iris is threatened due to shoreline development by residential and vacation homes, as well as the widening of roads and addition of chemical sprays and salts to roads. If you see this flower thriving in the wild, please don't pick it.

Here are **6** Dwarf Lake Iris flowers
we like them very much,
when you see them in the sand
look but please don't touch!

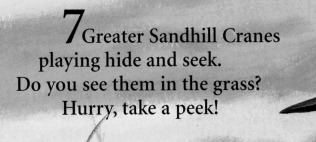

7 Greater Sandhill Cranes
playing hide and seek.
Do you see them in the grass?
Hurry, take a peek!

You can count
And let's not wait
To turn the page for number...

The Greater Sandhill Crane is a sub-species of a Sandhill Crane, which happens to be the world's oldest living species of bird. At 4 to 5 feet tall, the Greater Sandhill Crane has a wingspan of nearly 7 feet! This type of crane likes to eat worms, mice, frogs as well as grains. In Michigan, the Greater Sandhill Crane likes to take refuge during migration at Baker Sanctuary, in Calhoun County. Can you compare the wingspan of a crane to other objects that might be 7 feet long?

7

Michigan is the second leading producer of plantation-grown Christmas trees in the United States. This means that approximately 1 in 6 trees used in every home in the United States was grown in our state. Some of the most popular types are white pine, balsam, Douglas and Fraser fir, as well as the Colorado Blue and White spruce trees. It takes 7 years for a seedling to grow to the size of an average Christmas tree.

8 pretty Christmas trees
ready to be found,
bring them home and dress them up
with garland all around!

The Brook Trout is the official state fish of Michigan. It likes to swim in shallow rivers, lakes, and streams, and has brightly colored spots on its sides. In 1965, the trout was designated as Michigan's official state fish, but it wasn't until 1988 when the legislature specified which type of trout, the brook, should be the state symbol. Can you count the spots on each fish?

9 shiny brook trout
jumping with a swish.
Have you ever wished
for a polka-dotted fish?

Voyageurs are an important part of Michigan's past. In the 1800s, these French men traded beads, guns, and other goods with native American people for furs—primarily beaver furs. They traveled in large, heavy birchbark canoes, often with 5 or more men paddling with cedar paddles. They wore brightly colored clothes and were known for singing while they paddled and while they portaged.

10 red-capped voyageurs
sing a favorite song,
as they paddle through the water
they are swift and strong.

10

The fertile farmland of Michigan's thumb area is perfect for growing beans. So much so that the thumb area grows more beans than any other place in our country. Michigan grows 8 types of commercial classes of beans, some of which are navy, small white, black turtle, pinto, and light kidney beans. However, more than half of the beans produced in our state are navy beans.

11 tasty navy beans
sitting on a plate.
Would you like to taste them?
Mmmmm...they taste great!

Michigan is famous for its production of maple syrup. It ranks seventh in the United States for its production, and it averages about 80,000 gallons per year. It takes approximately 40 gallons of maple sap, which comes from the maple tree, to make 1 gallon of maple syrup. If you were to buy a ½ gallon of syrup, how many gallons of sap did it take to make that?

12 jugs of maple syrup,
it's so thick and sweet.
Pour it on your pancakes
for a yummy breakfast treat.

You count so well
and we are glad
Now let's try to COUNT and to ADD!

2 Karner Blue butterflies
resting near the shore

and 2 Kirtland's Warblers

can you count all **4?**

2+2=4

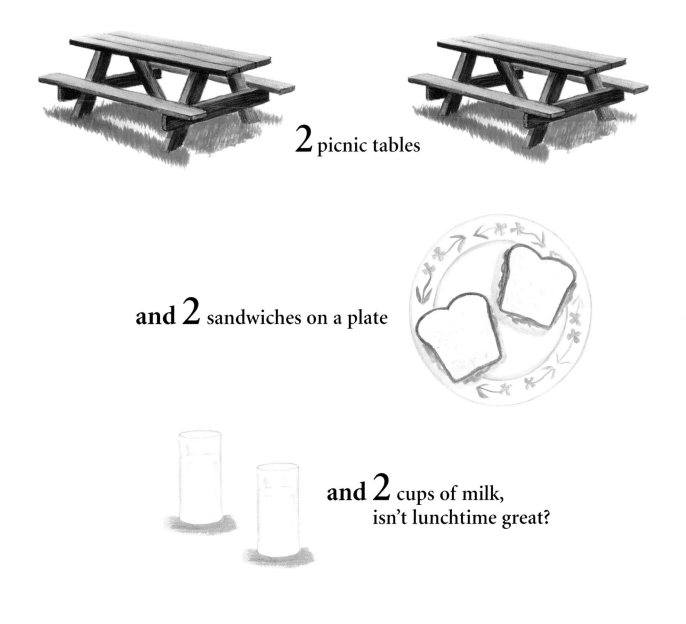

2 picnic tables

and 2 sandwiches on a plate

and 2 cups of milk,
isn't lunchtime great?

2+2+2=6

The Bald Eagle was generally distributed in Michigan in the early 1900s. However, a decline in the mid-1900s saw their numbers crash to near extinction due to loss of habitat and increased use of pesticides. As a Michigan endangered species, our national symbol likes to nest near shorelines, as fish are their main source of food. In Michigan, they can be seen in the winter in nearly all counties, but their population is concentrated in the Upper Peninsula and the Northern Lower Peninsula.

The Piping Plover is an endangered species, and very special to Michigan. All of the Great Lakes Piping Plovers were believed to have nested only in Michigan until in 1998, when one pair was discovered in Wisconsin. This small shorebird with a sandy-colored body likes wide, flat sandy beaches with little grass or vegetation. The nest of the Piping Plover is a shallow pebble-lined nest.

2 Greater Sandhill Cranes

and **2** Piping Plovers, too.

2 Whitetailed deer

and 2 Bald Eagles
staring back at you!

Can you count them?
That is great!
Add them up and you'll have **8!**

2+2+2+2=8

2 small Petoskey Stones

and 2 Painted Turtles on the beach,

2 lighthouses

and 2 sailboats

and 2 swans swimming out of reach.

$$2+2+2+2+2=10$$

Michigan has more lighthouses than any other state. The first lighthouse, Fort Gratiot Light on Lake Huron, was built in 1825.

The Petoskey Stone is the official state stone of Michigan. It is a fossil that is nearly 250 million years old, and the Painted Turtle is the official state reptile of Michigan. But that is not where the fun ends. Michigan has more registered boats than any other state in the country, with more than 900,000 boats registered.

The Mute Swan or White Swan, can be found in low wetland areas and around Lake Michigan. This bird will breed when it is 3 years old, and will have 3 to 8 eggs. It takes 35 days from the time the last egg is laid to the time they begin hatching. When the babies are born, they are gray but will turn to white. They will be able to fly in 3 to 4 months, but will stay with their parents until it is time for the next breeding season. This type of swan has been known to live over 25 years, but most of them live only 5 or 6 years.

Now see **3** moose a-wandering,

3 lady's slippers in the great U.P.,

and 3 white pines

and 3 waterfalls

there is so much for us to see.

$$3+3+3+3=12$$

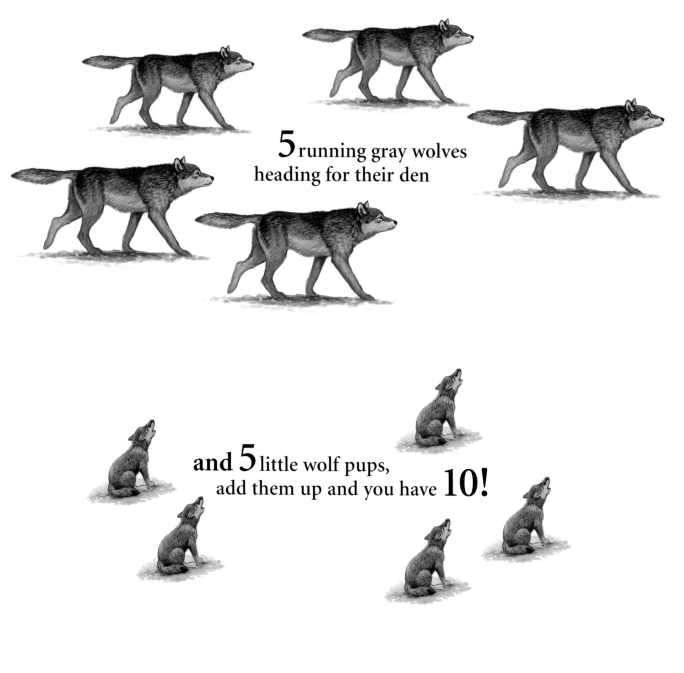

5 running gray wolves heading for their den

and 5 little wolf pups, add them up and you have **10!**

5+5=10

10 jugs of maple syrup
oh so sweet and plenty

and 10 tulips on the table
can you count to **20?**

Very good! We are at the end,
it's fun to count with you my friend,

so keep on counting what you see
it's Michigan numbers, **1-2-3!**

10+10=20

Kathy-jo Wargin

Author Kathy-jo Wargin loves to read and write, and count! She is the author of The Legend Series, which includes such classics as *The Legend of Sleeping Bear*, *The Legend of Mackinac Island*, and *The Legend of the Loon*. She has also written *M is for Mitten: A Michigan Alphabet*, *L is for Lincoln: An Illinois Alphabet*, *The Great Lakes Cottage Book* and *Michigan: The Spirit of the Land*. She lives in northern Michigan on 5 acres of woods with her loving family of 3, as well as 1 great dog, 4 cluttered desks, and thousands of stories in her heart.

Michael Glenn Monroe

Illustrator Michael Monroe's first painting was of a snow-white winter mink. His father later teased him that he'd drawn "the skinniest polar bear" he'd ever seen. Undaunted, Michael honed his craft through the years, teaching himself new techniques, becoming a renowned wildlife artist and the winner of the 1997 Michigan Duck Stamp award. His first two children's books, *M is for Mitten: A Michigan Alphabet* and *Buzzy the bumblebee*, took him to schools throughout the state, teaching school children simple shapes and techniques they can use to begin drawing. He recently released *A Wish To Be a Christmas Tree*, written by wife, Colleen. Michael also illustrated *S is for Sunshine: A Florida Alphabet*, due to be released in the fall of 2000. The Monroes reside in Brighton with their twins, Matthew and Natalie.